BIOGRAP

CW00502448

ALAN ARKIN

The Story Of A Remarkable Figure in The World of Entertainment—An Enigmatic a Artist Who Has Left an Indelible Mark on Stage and Screen

Nora Ivey Press

Copyright © 2023 NORA IVEY PRESS

All rights reserved. No part of this publication may be reproduced, distributed, or transmitted in any form or by any means, including photocopying, recording, or other electronic or mechanical methods, without the prior written permission of the publisher, except in the case of brief quotations embodied in critical reviews and certain other noncommercial uses permitted by copyright law.

This book is for educational and informational purposes only. It is not intended as a substitute for professional advice. The reader should always consult their professional advisors on any matter relating to their health, business, or personal life.

Table of Contents:

Chapter Ten:Conclusion: Unraveling the Enigma of Alan Arkin

Introduction: The Enigmatic Artist

Alan Arkin is a remarkable figure in the world of entertainment—an enigmatic artist who has left an indelible mark on stage and screen. Born on March 26, 1934, in Brooklyn, New York, Arkin's early years and family background played a crucial role in shaping his artistic sensibilities.

Early Years and Family Background

Alan Arkin was born to parents David and Beatrice Arkin, both of whom were passionate about the arts. His father, a painter, and writer, instilled in young Alan a deep appreciation for creativity and self-expression. Growing up in a culturally rich environment, Arkin was exposed to music, theater, and literature from an early age.

Despite the artistic influences at home, Arkin's childhood wasn't without its challenges. His family faced financial difficulties, leading to frequent moves and a sense of instability. These early struggles, however, instilled in Arkin resilience and a drive to succeed in his chosen path.

A Glimpse into Arkin's Persona

Arkin's persona is an intriguing blend of complexity, intensity, and a playful charm. Known for his intense performances and subtle humor, he possesses a unique ability to captivate audiences in a multitude of ways. Behind his enigmatic façade lies a deep well of emotions, which he fearlessly channels into his roles.

Arkin's introspective nature and dedication to his craft have earned him a reputation as a highly respected actor. Throughout his career, he has consistently sought out challenging and unconventional roles, refusing to be typecast or confined by expectations. This willingness to embrace the unexpected has allowed him to carve a distinctive niche in the entertainment industry.

In this biography, we will delve into the life and career of Alan Arkin, exploring the pivotal moments that shaped him as an artist. From his early struggles to his breakthrough on Broadway and his enduring impact on film, we will uncover the layers of this enigmatic artist, shedding light on the fascinating journey of Alan Arkin.

Chapter One:Discovering the Craft

The Call to Acting

Alan Arkin's journey as an actor began with a profound and undeniable call to the craft. From a young age, he felt a magnetic pull toward the world of theater and performance. Inspired by the captivating portrayals he witnessed on stage and screen, Arkin knew that acting was his true calling.

Training and Education

To hone his skills and immerse himself in the art of acting, Arkin pursued formal training and education. He enrolled at Bennington College in Vermont, where he studied theater and received invaluable guidance from seasoned instructors. It was during his time at Bennington that Arkin began to develop his unique approach to acting, blending his instincts with a deep understanding of the craft.

Arkin's education extended beyond the classroom as he sought out diverse experiences to enhance his skills. He immersed himself in the vibrant theater scene of New York City, attending performances and studying the work of established actors. This voracious appetite for knowledge and growth laid the foundation for his future success.

Early-Stage Performances

Arkin's journey as a performer took its initial steps on the stage. He embarked on a series of early-stage performances that allowed him to refine his craft and showcase his talents. These formative experiences helped shape his artistic sensibilities and provided him with invaluable opportunities to develop his acting range.

During this period, Arkin appeared in Off-Broadway productions, experimental theater projects, and regional theater productions. These diverse experiences exposed him to a variety of acting styles, genres, and creative collaborations. Each performance was a stepping stone, allowing Arkin to deepen his understanding of the craft and cultivate his distinct approach to acting.

As Arkin's talent became increasingly evident, his early-stage performances garnered critical acclaim and opened doors for further opportunities. The foundation he laid during these formative years would serve as the bedrock for his future success in both theater and film.

In the next chapters of this biography, we will delve into Arkin's breakthrough on Broadway and his transition to the silver screen, exploring the pivotal moments that propelled him into the spotlight and solidified his position as a formidable actor.

Chapter Two:A Breakthrough on Broadway

Arkin's ascent in the world of acting reached new heights with his breakthrough on Broadway. His remarkable talent and magnetic stage presence captivated audiences and critics alike, propelling him into the spotlight as a force to be reckoned with.

Notable Theater Roles

"Enter Laughing"

One of Arkin's early notable theater roles that brought him considerable attention was in the play "Enter Laughing." Based on the semi-autobiographical novel by Carl Reiner, the comedy depicted the trials and tribulations of a young aspiring actor in New York City. Arkin's portrayal of the lead character, David Kolowitz, showcased his impeccable comedic timing and charismatic stage presence. The production was a resounding success, earning critical acclaim and establishing Arkin as a rising star on Broadway.

"The Owl and the Pussycat"

Continuing his success on Broadway, Arkin secured a prominent role in the play "The Owl and the Pussycat." This Neil Simon comedy-drama delved into the unlikely relationship between a neurotic writer and a lively prostitute. Arkin's portrayal of the writer, Felix, showcased his versatility as an actor, seamlessly transitioning between comedic moments and poignant introspection. His chemistry with his co-star garnered praise, and the play became another milestone in Arkin's burgeoning career.

"Luv"

In the play "Luv," Arkin demonstrated his ability to navigate the complexities of dark comedy. The play, written by Murray Schisgal, explored the intricacies of love and relationships with sharp wit and humor. Arkin's performance as Harry, a man contemplating suicide, struck a delicate balance between comedy and vulnerability. His nuanced portrayal earned critical acclaim and further cemented his reputation as a versatile and accomplished actor.

Arkin's notable theater roles not only showcased his exceptional talent but also provided a platform for him to develop his skills and artistry. His performances on Broadway were a testament to his ability to captivate audiences and his versatility as an actor, setting the stage for his remarkable journey into the world of film and the further success that lay ahead.

In the upcoming chapters of this biography, we will explore Arkin's silver screen debut and delve into the diverse range of roles that have defined his career in film.

Chapter Three:The Silver Screen Debut

Arkin's transition from the stage to the silver screen marked a significant milestone in his career. With his distinctive blend of intensity and humor, he made an immediate impact in the world of cinema, leaving an indelible impression on audiences and critics alike.

Early Film Roles

"The Russians Are Coming, the Russians Are Coming"

In 1966, Arkin made his memorable film debut in the comedy-drama "The Russians Are Coming, the Russians Are Coming." Directed by Norman Jewison, the film followed the hilarious misadventures of a Soviet submarine crew that accidentally runs aground on a New England island. Arkin's portrayal of Lieutenant Yuri Rozanov, a Russian naval officer caught in a web of misunderstandings and comic situations, showcased his impeccable comedic timing and ability to infuse depth into his character. His performance earned critical acclaim and garnered him an Academy Award nomination for Best Actor, launching his film career on a high note.

"Wait Until Dark"

Arkin further showcased his versatility in the 1967 thriller "Wait Until Dark." Starring alongside Audrey Hepburn, he played the role of Roat, a menacing criminal who terrorizes a blind woman in her own home. Arkin's chilling performance as the cunning and ruthless antagonist demonstrated his ability to portray complex and sinister characters. His portrayal earned him widespread praise and demonstrated his range as an actor beyond comedy.

"Catch-22"

In 1970, Arkin delivered a standout performance in the war satire "Catch-22," based on Joseph Heller's novel. Directed by Mike Nichols, the film explored the absurdity and bureaucracy of war through the eyes of Captain Yossarian, played by Arkin. His portrayal of the disillusioned and morally conflicted airman encapsulated the dark humor and poignant social commentary of the story. Arkin's performance in "Catch-22" solidified his reputation as a skilled dramatic actor, adept at tackling complex characters and narratives.

These early film roles established Arkin as a versatile and compelling actor in the world of cinema. His ability to seamlessly transition between comedy and drama, and to infuse his characters with depth and authenticity, set him apart as a formidable talent. As we continue to explore Arkin's career in the following chapters, we will delve into his notable performances and the impact he made in the world of film.

Chapter Four:Comedic Genius

Alan Arkin's comedic brilliance has brought joy and laughter to audiences throughout his career. With his impeccable timing, subtle wit, and unparalleled ability to deliver humorous performances, he has cemented his status as a comedic genius. Let's explore some of Arkin's unforgettable comedy roles.

Unforgettable Comedy Performances

"The In-Laws"

In the 1979 comedy film "The In-Laws," Arkin starred alongside Peter Falk, delivering a comedic tour de force. Arkin portrayed Sheldon Kornpett, a conservative dentist who gets entangled in a whirlwind adventure when his daughter's soon-to-be father-in-law, played by Falk, reveals himself as a crazed CIA agent. Arkin's portrayal of the bewildered and increasingly exasperated Sheldon showcased his ability to navigate hilarious situations with deadpan humor. His chemistry with Falk created a dynamic and uproarious on-screen partnership, making "The In-Laws" a beloved comedy classic.

"Inspector Clouseau"

Arkin added his unique touch to the character of Inspector Clouseau in the 1968 film "Inspector Clouseau." Taking over the role originated by Peter Sellers, Arkin brought his charm and comedic sensibilities to the bumbling and accident-prone detective. Arkin's portrayal of

Clouseau showcased his physical comedy skills and ability to find humor in the most unexpected situations, creating a memorable and endearing interpretation of the character.

"Little Miss Sunshine"

Arkin's performance in the 2006 comedy-drama "Little Miss Sunshine" demonstrated his ability to blend humor with heartfelt emotion. Portraying the character of Edwin Hoover, the foul-mouthed yet lovable grandfather of a dysfunctional family, Arkin delivered a standout performance that earned him an Academy Award nomination for Best Supporting Actor. His comedic timing and poignant portrayal added depth and humanity to the film, contributing to its critical and commercial success.

These are just a few examples of Arkin's comedic genius, but his repertoire of memorable comedy performances extends far beyond. Whether through his wit, physicality, or nuanced delivery, Arkin's comedic talents have left an indelible mark on the genre. His ability to make audiences laugh while infusing his characters with depth and authenticity sets him apart as a true comedic icon.

In the upcoming chapters, we will continue to explore Arkin's career and delve into his remarkable performances in both comedic and dramatic roles, further unraveling the multifaceted talent of this extraordinary actor.

Chapter Five:Embracing Dramatic Depths

While Alan Arkin's comedic prowess is widely celebrated, he has also delved into dramatic roles with remarkable depth and complexity. His ability to inhabit complex characters and explore the depths of human emotion has garnered critical acclaim and further showcased his exceptional talent. Let's explore some of Arkin's memorable dramatic performances.

Exploring Complex Characters

"The Heart Is a Lonely Hunter"

In the 1968 film adaptation of Carson McCullers' novel "The Heart Is a Lonely Hunter," Arkin delivered a profoundly moving performance. Portraying John Singer, a deaf-mute man who becomes a confidant to various troubled individuals in a small Southern town, Arkin conveyed a sense of quiet strength and empathy. His portrayal showcased his ability to communicate through subtle gestures and expressions, capturing the essence of the character's loneliness and longing for connection. Arkin's nuanced performance earned him an Academy Award nomination for Best Actor and solidified his reputation as a formidable dramatic actor.

"Glengarry Glen Ross"

Arkin's role as George Aaronow in the 1992 film adaptation of David Mamet's play "Glengarry Glen Ross" demonstrated his ability to navigate the complex dynamics of an ensemble cast. The film explored the cutthroat world of real estate salesmen, and Arkin's portrayal of the meek and downtrodden Aaronow added a layer of vulnerability to the character. His performance alongside an ensemble of esteemed actors showcased his ability to hold his own in intense and emotionally charged scenes, earning him critical acclaim.

"Argo"

In the 2012 political thriller "Argo," directed by Ben Affleck, Arkin portrayed Hollywood producer Lester Siegel. The film, based on true events, centered around the covert operation to rescue

Americans during the Iran hostage crisis. Arkin's performance as Siegel, a seasoned and cynical film industry veteran, added a touch of levity and wit to the intense narrative. His portrayal captured the character's savvy and resilience, providing a refreshing contrast to the tension-filled plot. Arkin's performance contributed to the film's success and earned him an Academy Award nomination for Best Supporting Actor.

Arkin's ability to delve into the dramatic depths of complex characters is a testament to his range and versatility as an actor. Whether embodying the quiet strength of a misunderstood protagonist or adding depth to an ensemble, he brings authenticity and emotional depth to his performances.

As we continue to explore Arkin's career in the following chapters, we will delve further into his remarkable dramatic performances and the impact he has made in the world of film.

Chapter Six:Behind the Camera: Directing and Writing

Alan Arkin's creative talents extend beyond acting, as he has also ventured into the realms of directing, writing, and producing. With a keen eye for storytelling and a desire to explore different facets of the filmmaking process, Arkin has left his mark behind the camera as well. Let's explore his endeavors in directing and writing.

Venturing into Directing

"Little Murders"

In 1971, Arkin made his directorial debut with the dark comedy film "Little Murders," based on Jules Feiffer's play. Arkin's directorial style brought a unique vision to the screen, combining biting social commentary with absurdist humor. The film, set in a dystopian and violent New York City, delved into the disconnection and chaos of urban life. Arkin's directorial debut showcased his ability to create a distinct atmosphere and draw out nuanced performances from the cast, further establishing his creative prowess beyond acting.

"The Four Seasons"

Arkin continued his directorial journey with the 1981 comedy-drama film "The Four Seasons." In addition to directing, he also wrote and starred in the film. "The Four Seasons" explored the dynamics of three couples who vacation together regularly throughout the year, navigating the complexities of relationships, friendships, and personal growth. Arkin's direction captured the emotional nuances of the characters and their evolving dynamics, showcasing his ability to balance humor and heartfelt moments. The film's critical success demonstrated Arkin's skill as both a director and writer.

Writing and Producing Projects

Arkin's involvement in the filmmaking process extended beyond directing. He has also showcased his writing and producing talents in various projects. While not all of these ventures were widely known, they highlighted Arkin's multifaceted creative abilities.

Arkin's experiences and insights as an actor and artist undoubtedly informed his writing and producing endeavors. His understanding of character development, storytelling, and the craft of filmmaking allowed him to contribute to the creative process from multiple angles, further solidifying his reputation as a versatile and multifaceted talent.

In the following chapters of this biography, we will continue to explore Arkin's remarkable career and delve into his notable achievements as an actor, director, and writer.

Chapter Seven: Life Beyond Acting

While Alan Arkin is renowned for his contributions to the world of acting and filmmaking, his life extends beyond the glitz and glamour of Hollywood. In this chapter, we delve into his relationships, struggles, and triumphs, as well as his activism and philanthropic endeavors.

Personal Relationships and Family

Arkin's personal life has been marked by significant relationships and a close-knit family. He has been married three times, with his current wife, Suzanne Newlander, whom he married in 1996. Arkin has three sons: Adam, Matthew, and Anthony, who have all followed in their father's footsteps and pursued careers in the entertainment industry. Arkin's family has been a source of support and inspiration throughout his journey, and their bond remains an essential aspect of his life.

Personal Struggles and Triumphs

Like many individuals in the public eye, Arkin has faced personal struggles throughout his life. He has been open about his battles with anxiety and stage fright, which have impacted him at various points in his career. However, Arkin's resilience and determination have allowed him to overcome these challenges and continue to deliver exceptional performances.

In addition to his struggles, Arkin has celebrated numerous triumphs throughout his life. From his critically acclaimed performances to his directorial achievements, he has received accolades and recognition for his contributions to the arts. These triumphs stand as a testament to his talent, hard work, and dedication.

Activism and Philanthropy

Arkin's commitment to social and political causes is evident in his activism and philanthropic efforts. He has been a vocal advocate for peace and nuclear disarmament, speaking out against war and advocating for nonviolent solutions.

Arkin has also supported various charitable organizations and causes, using his platform and resources to make a positive impact on society.

His passion for social justice extends beyond his acting career, demonstrating his dedication to making a difference in the world beyond the realm of entertainment.

As we explore Arkin's life beyond acting, we gain a deeper understanding of the man behind the characters. His personal relationships, triumphs, and struggles have shaped him as an individual, while his activism and philanthropy reflect his desire to make a positive impact on the world.

In the following chapters, we will continue to uncover more about Arkin's life and career, delving into his later works and the legacy he has created in the world of entertainment and beyond.

Chapter Eight: Accolades and Recognition

Throughout his illustrious career, Alan Arkin has received numerous accolades and recognition for his exceptional talent and contributions to the world of acting. From prestigious awards to industry honors, his work has been celebrated by his peers and critics alike. In this chapter, we explore the noteworthy accolades and achievements that highlight Arkin's remarkable career.

Academy Awards and Nominations

Arkin's talent has been acknowledged by the Academy of Motion Picture Arts and Sciences on multiple occasions. He has received several Academy Award nominations and took home the coveted golden statuette for his outstanding performances.

In 1967, Arkin received his first Academy Award nomination for Best Actor for his role in "The Russians Are Coming, the Russians Are Coming." The following year, he received a second nomination in the same category for his poignant portrayal in "The Heart Is a Lonely Hunter."

Arkin's third Academy Award nomination came in 2007 for Best Supporting Actor in the film "Little Miss Sunshine." His portrayal of the eccentric and lovable grandfather earned him critical acclaim and the coveted Oscar.

Golden Globe Awards

Arkin's talent has also been recognized by the Hollywood Foreign Press Association, earning him Golden Globe Awards and nominations.

In 1968, Arkin received a Golden Globe nomination for Best Actor - Motion Picture Drama for his role in "The Heart Is a Lonely Hunter." He then went on to win the Golden Globe for Best Actor - Motion Picture Musical or Comedy in 1969 for his performance in "The Russians Are Coming, the Russians Are Coming."

Arkin's exceptional performance in "Little Miss Sunshine" garnered him a Golden Globe nomination for Best Supporting Actor in 2007, further solidifying his reputation as a versatile and accomplished actor.

Other Honors and Achievements

Beyond the Academy Awards and Golden Globe recognition, Arkin has been the recipient of several other honors and achievements. In 2002, he was awarded a star on the Hollywood Walk of Fame, a testament to his enduring impact on the entertainment industry.

Arkin's work has also been recognized by various critics' associations and film festivals. He has received accolades from the Screen Actors Guild Awards, BAFTA Awards, and the Cannes Film

Festival, among others. These honors reflect the high regard in which his talent is held within the industry.

Arkin's legacy as an exceptional actor and artist is not only measured by awards and accolades but also by the lasting impact he has made on the world of film and his influence on future generations of actors.

As we continue to explore Arkin's life and career, we uncover more about his remarkable contributions and the enduring legacy he has created in the realm of acting and beyond.

Chapter Nine:Reflecting on a Legacy

Alan Arkin's extraordinary career and contributions to the acting industry have left an indelible mark on both his peers and future generations of actors. As we reflect on his legacy, we recognize the significant impact he has made, his influence on aspiring performers, and his continued artistic contributions.

Impact on the Acting Industry

Arkin's impact on the acting industry is profound, characterized by his versatility, authenticity, and unwavering commitment to his craft. His ability to seamlessly transition between comedic and dramatic roles, his impeccable timing, and his ability to bring complex characters to life has set a standard of excellence in the profession.

Arkin's commitment to authenticity and honesty in his performances has inspired actors worldwide to delve deeper into their characters and push the boundaries of their craft. His work serves as a reminder of the power of storytelling and the transformative nature of acting.

Influence on Future Generations

Arkin's influence on future generations of actors cannot be overstated. Through his performances, he has demonstrated the importance of versatility, dedication, and fearlessness in embracing diverse roles. Many aspiring actors look to Arkin as a source of inspiration, learning from his nuanced performances, and incorporating elements of his style into their work.

Arkin's impact extends beyond his on-screen performances. As a director, writer, and producer, he has shown aspiring artists the possibilities of multidimensional careers and encouraged them to explore different facets of the filmmaking process. His willingness to take creative risks and explore new territories has inspired countless individuals to follow their artistic instincts.

Continuing Artistic Contributions

Even after several decades in the industry, Arkin continues to make significant artistic contributions. He remains an active and sought-after actor, always bringing something fresh and captivating to his roles. His commitment to excellence and his dedication to his craft has not wavered, ensuring that his artistic legacy continues to evolve.

Arkin's creative journey goes beyond acting, as he continues to write, direct, and produce projects that captivate audiences and push artistic boundaries. His willingness to explore new avenues of storytelling and his passion for the craft serves as an inspiration for artists at all stages of their careers.

As we reflect on Arkin's legacy, we recognize the profound impact he has made on the acting industry, the influence he has had on future generations, and his ongoing artistic contributions. His body of work stands as a testament to his talent, passion, and unwavering dedication to his art.

Chapter Ten:Conclusion: Unraveling the Enigma of Alan Arkin

Alan Arkin's career and life are as enigmatic as they are remarkable. From his early beginnings to his enduring legacy, Arkin has captivated audiences with his versatility, authenticity, and unwavering dedication to his craft. Through his performances, he has taken us on a journey, inviting us to explore the depths of human emotion and the intricacies of the human experience.

Throughout this biography, we have traced Arkin's journey from his early years and family background to his breakthrough on Broadway, his silver screen debut, and his unforgettable comedic and dramatic performances. We have also explored his ventures into directing, writing, and producing, as well as his relationships, struggles, and triumphs.

Arkin's career is marked by an impressive array of accolades, including Academy Awards, Golden Globe Awards, and recognition from prestigious organizations. His impact on the acting industry is undeniable, inspiring aspiring actors and leaving an indelible mark on the craft.

But Arkin's legacy extends beyond awards and accolades. He has influenced future generations of performers through his dedication to authenticity, his willingness to take creative risks, and his ability to infuse each character with depth and complexity. His work serves as a testament to the power of storytelling and the transformative nature of the arts.

As we unravel the enigma of Alan Arkin, we discover a multifaceted artist who defies categorization. He seamlessly transitions between comedy and drama, effortlessly capturing the essence of each character he portrays. Behind the camera, he showcases his creative vision as a director and writer, enriching the artistic landscape with his unique perspective.

Arkin's contributions to the arts go beyond the stage and screen. His activism and philanthropy reflect his commitment to making a positive impact on the world, advocating for peace, and supporting various charitable causes.

As we conclude this biography, we are left with a profound appreciation for the enigmatic artist that is Alan Arkin. His talent, passion, and unwavering dedication to his craft have shaped a remarkable career that continues to inspire and captivate audiences. Arkin's legacy as an actor, director, writer, and philanthropist will endure, leaving an indelible mark on the world of entertainment and beyond.

Through his performances and creative endeavors, Arkin invites us to reflect on our humanity, embrace the complexities of life, and find meaning in the stories we tell. He reminds us of the power of art to inspire, transform, and connect us, transcending boundaries and unraveling the enigma of what it means to be human.

Alan Arkin, the enigmatic artist, continues to leave an indelible imprint on the world, reminding us of the timeless power of storytelling and the enduring impact of a true master of his craft.

THE END

Printed in Great Britain
by Amazon

34709071R00046